The Man Commandments

A book on etiquette, grooming, responsibility and relationships.

Written by:
Michael Siekiem-Kontom McKinney
PKA Siekiem-Kontom

Copyright © 2019

All rights reserved.
International Standard Book Number:
978-0-578-53752-8

This book or parts thereof may not be reproduced in any form, stored in a retrieval system or transmitted in any form by any means, electronic, mechanical, photocopying, recording, or otherwise, without prior written permission of the publisher except as provided by United States Copyright Law.

TABLE OF CONTENTS

The Man Commandments	4
The Author's Insight	6
Introduction	9
Chapter 1 Three is the magic number	12
Chapter 2 A Father's Worth	25
Chapter 3 The Basics 101	32
Chapter 4 Wipe Your Feet At The Door	40
Chapter 5 NOW!	49
Chapter 6 Man Vs. Woman	54
Chapter 7 Chivalry Isn't Dead	64
Chapter 8 Black Love	71
Conclusion	78
Dedication	79
Acknowledgements	82

The Man Commandments

THE MAN COMMANDMENTS

Here before you are 10 commandments every young man and men of all ages should live by.

1. Believe and surrender to a higher power. Having a connection with the Most High i.e. your (enlightened self) is the ONLY way.

2. Walk upright, honest and respectful. Positive energy transforms into positive outcomes.

3. Take care of your family, (children) and spouse. Do not create a world in which you abandon or neglect.

4. Be mindful of your behavior. Men are the foundation and backbones of our society. One who acts unlike a leader cannot lead.

5. Speak with conviction and intellect. A knowledgeable man is a man of substance.

6. Love with everything that is in you. Give that love without rationing anything of you.

7. Whenever in conflict think wisely before you opt for war. A mind that surpasses its opposition is the victor.

8. Live so the future of others may prosper from your contributions to world. When you live in vain you destroy your legacy and hope for the young.

9. Live with a purpose, die for a cause. To walk this earth without direction is to shame self and the creator.

The Man Commandments

10. Love life for life is for the living. Acknowledge all that is, for they are all blessings. Whether good or bad, life's experiences shape us to be better people.

~ Siekiem-Kontom

The Man Commandments

The Author's Insight

A gentleman asked a distinguished elder if it was absolutely safe to wear suede shoes in the rain. The distinguished elder responded, "Son, have you ever seen a cow with an umbrella? Of course you can wear suede in the rain." The gentleman chuckled and said "Sir, You have made an odd yet humorous point there." The distinguished elder went on to respond "The tale about not wearing suede shoes in the rain was started by someone with only one pair of suede shoes. You can't allow one incident to predict the outcome of your future." The gentleman nodded in agreement. He went on to ask, "This isn't just about shoes, is it?" ~ SK

The analogy with the cow in the rain and suede shoes is merely to make a point. We are born with the ability to adapt and weather different conditions placed upon us. Regardless of whom or what. The issues we face in life may become extremely difficult at times. No matter what,

The Man Commandments

you can and shall stand the rain. Never allow one incident to distract you from showing the world your greatness.

Remind yourself on a daily basis that you are forever evolving, forever growing. In the chapters that I have compiled, they are to serve as a guide for the young men and Man of today. In a climate where social status has taken hold of the identity of manhood and masculinity, I felt a dire need to address my fellow man on a more interpersonal level. Basically, an old school chat with my brothers if you will. In the following chapters I ask that you read and embrace with an open mind and heart. Whether you read this book once or a hundred times, I want every single word to resonate and bring about change where change is needed.

Honestly, I did not plan for my thoughts to manifest into books for the world's review. Now that I am here, my sole

The Man Commandments

purpose is to share my perspective and I will not be compromised. An honest approach shall bring forth honest results in my opinion. I truly believe that it is my duty to speak my peace and bring forth change. As a man it is my duty to uplift, support, and guide another. This is the only way to ensure accountability and nobility amongst the ranks.

So if they ask what is the purpose of this book, you tell them it is to provide a different narrative of today's man. This book was written to bring about a sense of clarity where needed. I came to remove ego and bravado from the male's approach and tackle topics with truth and sincerity. This I believe is the only way.

The Man Commandments

Introduction

The greatest thing about life is that YOU are the sole controller behind what is said, written, and thought of about you. You are the MASTER of your destiny. Never allow an outsider to define nor dictate to you YOUR path nor passion. Truth be told, many people have written me off. They doubted me. They questioned my purpose.

They may have even gone as far as to talk negatively about me. Despite it all my faith and belief in self never wavered. When you are sure and secure within yourself obstacles are minute. As easy as it were for people to write me off it was even easier to write myself back in. There is no other breathing entity greater than self. Therefore you MUST believe in yourself.

As I am, you are the MASTER of your destiny. Forget about what they said regarding you yesterday. Give them

The Man Commandments

something powerful to talk about TODAY. Regardless of your past, your future is a canvas awaiting your greatest creation. Use every opportunity given to take yourself to that next level.

Enrich yourself. Educate yourself and most importantly love yourself. Once you've embraced that inner power nothing can stop you from accomplishing anything your mind has set forth to do. You should never allow another person's limitations to become yours. Do the impossible. Become the unstoppable. Allow the words on these pages to guide you to your destination. Your future is waiting for you.

The Man Commandments

FOOD FOR THOUGHT

If you profess to be a man then be that. Your goal should be to become the profound definition and nature of a man's true character. Genitalia and facial hair are only defining factors of your anatomical and exterior composition. The way you live in accordance to order, respect, responsibility and accountability makes you a TRUE MAN.

The Man Commandments

Chapter One

Three is the magic number

(Education, Responsibility, Faith)

I feel that it is my responsibility as a person of the African American community to share some insight and guidance with those I share a kinship. I ask that you use these words as a manual to align yourself along the path of personal and intellectual growth. I will discuss three (3) components, which are as follows: education, responsibility and faith. Hopefully this information will become a guide and benefit you and your loved one's alike. Let's begin.

Education

My dear Brothers, it is imperative that you gravitate and embrace the concept of obtaining as much knowledge as possible. The dilemmas young men face today are mainly due to their lack of knowledge and their lack of drive. Another factor is they have little concern for their sense of

The Man Commandments

belonging in this society. There is a saying "If you knew better, you would do better". We laugh at this quote yet it hits home ever so often.

Our young men are caught in the matrix, an altered emotional and physical virtuality. An unrealistic state of being which appears to be real and rewarding but in essence isn't. For some, there is little to no desire to learn for they are convinced it will never pay off. I am here to tell you that this way of thinking is the furthest thing from the truth. Never allow the thought of not being well versed on a subject matter keep you from learning. Never sell yourself short because you do not have the financial means for a collegiate education.

Where there is a library there is knowledge. Do not allow society and naysayers to dictate how far you will go in life. Make the decision to seek knowledge, wisdom and

The Man Commandments

understanding by any means. A knowledgeable man is a leader. A man who embraces knowledge shall also embrace the responsibility that comes along with being in the knowing.

Whether you seek education by way of trade or college. One must always understand that education is the key to one's growth. Information obtained can never be taken away. This is why educating oneself is so important. The more knowledgeable you are the more value you add to yourself. The least you know the easier it is to replace you. This, my friend, is simple mathematics. Knowledge in today's society is a gem. It is most valuable, for what can be obtained by way of knowledge is limitless. The more you know the stronger you are. The stronger you are mentally the weaker your opposition and obstacles become. This gives you the courage to face any fight before you.

The Man Commandments

Knowledge is a sure guide to your dreams. It can propel you to heights unimaginable. Where doors are locked knowledge will open them. The reassurance and confidence that being knowledgeable gives is greater than anything you can adorn yourself with. No car, home, nor jewelry can compare to the value of a man in his right mind.

Responsibility

Many young men simply evade the word (responsibility) and the meaning all-together. Allow me to break this down in "real time". I shall elaborate in a way that I know my young brothers can relate. For starters, if you are 18 and residing in your parents/guardian home you must carry your OWN weight. Bottom line. You do yourself a disservice as a young man by not assuming the role of being responsible.

The Man Commandments

The idea of a 16-18 year old wanting to be treated as an adult, yet carries the attributes of a child, are far too common. Responsibility is not a one-way street pertaining to parent and child. The teenager has a responsibility as well within their household. More importantly these responsibilities must be reinforced.

Teenagers: This means upholding your academics. Making sure education remains a priority. If permissible, consider finding after school employment or part time job. A young man who is earning an income tends to value the things he buys with his own money. This teaches the young man a direct lesson on responsibility and the true value of a dollar.

In your home you should always clean up after yourself. You should also assist with grocery shopping and cooking. These are life's skills that will benefit you when you are more mature and out into the real world. Many young men

The Man Commandments

who live in their parents/guardian home think they are to be cared for and sheltered as an infant. This mindset and behavior will only cripple you.

When the day approaches when you believe you're at the age of moving out on your own you may not know how to efficiently survive. You may carry the basic tools instilled in you by your parents, meanwhile the ability to make decisions on your own regarding finances and medical may throw you for a loop. No one will be there to remind you that rent is due or how to properly sanitize your kitchen and bathroom.

Though some may shrug this off I have seen many succumb to the lack of these abilities in the worst way. This is basically due to the prolonging of a lifestyle where you are dependent upon another. You will carry on this trait for years unless you take responsibility for yourself NOW.

The Man Commandments

Young men, do not wait until you reach your 20's to learn how to take care of yourself. You may find yourself in an awkward and frustrating situation. In many cases, you're trying to catch up and adapt for all of the years you've wasted being naive.

Teenagers, or as you may like to be addressed, young men, ages 16-18 the time is NOW for you to get things into swing. You are at a defining point in your life. I ask that you do not take these years and the lessons that come along with them for granted. Set the tone for greatness now in order to enjoy the rewards later in life.

Being a teenager is a pivotal time in your life. These are the years of lessons, errors, heartbreak and adventure. Do not throw these years away by following the crowd. Focus on being an individual and carving out your own identity and

The Man Commandments

path in this society. The time is in your favor. Do not cheat the clock. You have to beat the clock.

Men: Accept responsibility for the world you have created. Whether it is a world of debt or a world of conflict. Assume your rightful position and take responsibility for EVERY action as well as inaction on your part. It is counter productive to complain about the mess that you're in without acknowledging and taking responsibility for placing yourself in this very situation. Stop lying to yourself by stating "things always seem to go wrong for me". Maybe, just maybe, you're doing something wrong. If you are not checking yourself and making an attempt to correct the error of your ways, conflict and confusion shall continue to follow you. Regardless of your financial situation, take care of the children you've partnered to bring into this world. Disliking your ex wife, ex-girlfriend is not a valid reason for neglecting your obligations.

The Man Commandments

We can all debate about the imbalance and bureaucracy of the child support system. One thing a man should never debate, nor attempt to justify, is neglecting his responsibilities as a parent. Your financial contributions should not be a trade off for time spent with your child and vice versa. Just as your children need to be reared and loved by you, they also require financial assistance.

There will always be some kind of financial burden upon the one paying child support. This goes without question. I ask that you imagine the burden placed upon your children without your assistance. I ask that you place ego aside and place the nurturing of your children first. The dollar amount contributed is not what makes you a man nor less of man. It is your willingness to be there for your children that will determine that.

The Man Commandments

Having any amount of animosity towards an ex will never make for a smooth relationship between you and your children and their welfare. Whether you get along with the mother of your children or not should not determine how much and how often you contribute to the care of the children. Being supportive is not an option you get to check off in a box on a piece of paper. Those children are real and they need your love, care and support in REAL TIME.

Faith

I come into contact with men from all walks of life. One thing that differentiates one from the other is how we internalize the things that affect our faith and us. Men without a sense of faith or belief in a Higher Power seem more hostile and agitated with various situations in my opinion. I believe this is because they see no end or resolution to their confusion. Those that may embrace the concept of a deeper meaning to life may appear a bit more resolved.

The Man Commandments

We understand that even though there is an issue it can, and will, be worked through. Taking a deeper look into ourselves and finding that inner strength is what pulls us through. Embracing the concept that YOU are the MASTER of SELF. This level of self-mastery will assist you from subjecting yourself to conflict.

The lack of faith and understanding in our young men may often lead to a feeling of hopelessness. This state of being is then compiled with the onset of depression, which may lead to our young brothers going astray. Knowledge of self and faith must be your foundation. Whether it be religion based, spirituality, or belief in self, you must know and live out this greater purpose.

Succumbing to anything negative and destructive is detrimental to your mental and physical health. This shall also effect how you engage and interact with others on an

The Man Commandments

emotional and spiritual level. My Brothers, I ask that you give yourself a fighting chance. Take pride in knowing you are a divine and powerful force.

You are the leaders of your family and the Universal community. Take pride in knowing this. Live righteous and just. You have a future of infinite possibilities. Do not allow it to pass you by. Believing in yourself can propel you to heights unimaginable. All it takes is for you to see yourself as who you truly are, a divine being created to bring forth beauty and greatness. Though many get lost along their way in finding themselves, trust and believe all that you need to succeed resides within you. You simply have to believe in yourself and never doubt your capabilities.

The Man Commandments

FOOD FOR THOUGHT

You cannot be enlightened and frightened at the same time.

To KNOW is to fully understand all probabilities. Whether you address them or suppress them, it is totally up to you.

The Man Commandments

Chapter Two

A Father's Worth

I would like to take this opportunity to acknowledge those of us men who have the great responsibility of being a father. Regardless of your financial situation, education and employment status, if you are committed to the rearing and well being of the lives you have partnered to bring into existence I salute you.

In a society where men struggle day in and day out to be great, being acknowledged as dedicated fathers is another topic in itself. The window that exposes the view of men of substance has become smaller.

The image of prominent and strong fathers has disappeared from television all together. I can remember the days when we could watch a particular television program and pick up a fashion tip or two from America's favorite Dad. We could

The Man Commandments

watch how a man/father showered affection towards his wife and children. Present time - we have television shows where men insult their wives and shun their children all in the name of comedy and brazen humor. Our society has made it customary for men to walk alone and not as a unit with woman & child. This is by all means an intentional division created by suggestive programming that makes it appear cool to be single, divorced and uncommitted.

You may have noticed the advertisements on billboards all around our communities. Ads that display men partying with their friends holding a glass of cognac, meanwhile any image of a Black father with his son or daughter is hard to find. I can thumb through countless magazines and find men in advertisements selling cigarettes, liquor, hair dye and cars. In contrast there are few magazine or television ads of men at the head of a table with their family, specifically black men. There are seldom advertisements of

The Man Commandments

men teaching a son or daughter to read or ride a bike. It is as if male parental figures are being wiped out of the public's view.

If you happen to run across an ad of a man with his family the ad is more than likely that of a biracial family. Ads in print or aired on television of men in a parental role either illustrate the men as being distressed or in need of some kind of medication. If it's not that, it's usually an ad ran near Father's Day and other holidays to subconsciously place the financial burden or responsibility on said father. This is systematically done that the imagery of Black men as Black fathers in Black households are far and few in between in the media.

All of the things that I've mentioned are the results of social analysis. We, Black Fathers, are considered to be absent and obsolete when it comes to the family nucleus. How do

The Man Commandments

we correct this? How do we become visible in a society that overlooks a large percentage of us?

When do we own up to our own fears and negligence and assume the position that is rightfully ours. Men must begin to be men again. We must strip away the false narrative of being cool and redefine what "cool" is. Cool is being productive and trust worthy. Cool is carrying one's self-upright and honorable.

Men, we must take responsibility for the energy we put forth into the universe. The words we use, the actions we display and the behavioral patterns we demonstrate. These actions tend to come back full circle with everything within our equation.

Therefore, if you are one that curses continuously, those that are immediately around you will pick up this habit. If

The Man Commandments

you are one to speak harshly to your wife or the mother of your children then eventually your children will respond the exact same way to her. In many cases they may also exhibit this behavior around others they come in contact with outside of the home. These are negative behavioral patterns we should never allow our children to perpetuate.

Instead, we should focus on aligning our children with positive reinforcements to equip them for their future. Being an example of a responsible and nurturing male role model is key. Take time out to learn fathering techniques. Learn how to listen to your children when they are describing their day in school, etc.

Take your daughters out for one on one time. Find out what her passions are and how she views the world around her and the people in it. Take your sons out to restaurants.

The Man Commandments

Teach them how to order from a menu and how to hold his eating utensils properly. Take your children to the museum.

Expose them to nature and the world's culture. Do not allow the next generation to be limited in knowledge. This prevents mental growth. By not allowing your children to broaden their horizon will only limit them. Being a great father does not mean cutting a check on a bi weekly or monthly basis.

Being a great father begins with you taking the initiative to create a world for your children that empowers them. Fill them with the enrichment of love and wisdom that only a father can give.

To the fathers throughout the world, may the Most High continue to bless you and guide you.

The Man Commandments

FOOD FOR THOUGHT

Stop believing that wearing a suit makes you soft. The person that worries about being mistaken as chump for wearing a suit is already a chump. Whether you're in a suit or Timberland boots, you are who you are. Stop being concerned about perception. It is your insecurities that will hold you back and keep you from meeting some great people.

The Man Commandments

Chapter Three

The Basics: 101

In the climate of colorful hair, facial tattoos, and an effeminate behavioral trend amongst our men, I have decided to share some sure tips to set you on the right path. Young men, you should be weary when looking towards your favorite artists or entertainers for business and fashion tips. They are not in the 9 to 5 world. The outfit that may appear to be cool for the party scene will not cut it if you plan on being a part of the work force and corporate bound.

This fascination with men being "flamboyant" by way of fashion hasn't been the proper code of conduct. Being unique and radical are two different things. You don't need to prove your individuality through fashion because you are already your own person. Embrace that for what it is THEN build around that. Going out of your way to stand out will only make many around you stand offish.

The Man Commandments

Men, always make it your business to properly clean your body and neatly press your attire to the best of your ability. A person that is not properly groomed is looked upon as being unprepared and unkempt. This is not acceptable in a professional setting. Wearing your attire in accordance to the social trends is not necessarily a wise decision unless you're in the fashion industry. Do not make money an excuse for your lack of concern for your own appearance. Regardless of income, one should make an effort to look the part of the position they desire to be.

Before heading out the door for the day every man should take a good look at himself before leaving his residence. Make sure everything is in the right place and neatly organized. When you become disorganized it takes away from your presentation and overall appearance. Taking pride in one's appearance should not be contingent on how much money you make. Pride and self esteem is something

The Man Commandments

we as men must posses before finances and attire comes into play.

When we as men possess these great traits it exudes through any garment we adorn. This, my friend, is the true embodiment of a man. What I am about to address is specifically directed for my young Brothers beginning in the work force. You should never and I repeat NEVER should you at any time travel to and from your place of business with a stocking cap, du-rag, head wrap (non religious), or any other hair wrap on your head. This has become very common yet unacceptable.

Take the appropriate time needed to tend to your appearance before departing your residence. Many young men are more concerned with maintaining the perfect wave pattern in their hair than their overall appearance.

The Man Commandments

Proper grooming of your hair is key. In close encounters we lead with two things, our handshake and our face. These two are the headers of any introduction. So while grooming of the hair is important. It is best to not be in the morning meeting with a fresh indentation in your forehead from a du-rag lace. Take the necessary measures in the morning to get yourself together. The man that's intact is the cool one.

Whoever said wearing their pants below their ass is stylish or keeping it real LIED TO YOU! This distorted fashion trend has taken over young men across the world. This fashion craze is nothing more than the expression of oneself in society. These young men find themselves as outsiders so in turn they appear as such. They have taken an appearance that began in the prison system and made it an urban fashion trend.

The Man Commandments

Inmates after going through the general intake process must have their belongings confiscated and exchanged for a prison outfit. On many occasions the outfits would not properly fit the inmates so their pants would sag off of them. Inmate's belts are confiscated just in case they are a suicide risk. In many cases depending on an inmate's mental evaluations, they are not allowed belts or shoelaces. Another claim to the sagging pants trend, which began in prison, is that homosexuals use it to advertise that their ass is available for possible takers (pun intended).

So I ask, this trend that many are into, is this the image you're intentionally giving off?

If you all know what is best I suggest you start wearing garments that are your actual size. Wearing slacks or shirts that are either too tight or too baggy are not proper attire for the work place depending on your line of work. Take time

The Man Commandments

and a few dollars to invest in tailoring at your local dry cleaners or a tailor. This can take you and your wardrobe a long way. A well-dressed person is more likely to be well respected in my humble opinion.

When it comes to a man's appearance it's cool to be noticeable but let's not over do it. Develop a sense of color schemes for your work attire that enhances your personality without going overboard. Bright and flashy garments are necessarily frowned upon and not favorable in various corporate office settings. Natural earth tones are preferably great to go with. That bright yellow shirt and orange tie is not corporate attire, unless you own the company and then can wear whatever you like.

My Brothers, this information was given to you for your own enlightenment. These words are not written with the intent to humiliate nor look down upon what you may be

The Man Commandments

accustomed to doing. Although we may believe something looks nice on us, we must realize that everything is NOT to be worn everywhere. We must use discretion and choose our attire wisely. Your first impression can open many doors or prevent them from opening at all. REMINDER: Timberlands, skully cap and bubble vest does not make you a thug. Just as a tie, tailored suit, and shined shoes does not make you a businessman. It is your character, focus and mind set that shall define you.

The Man Commandments

FOOD FOR THOUGHT

Be able to associate and converse with all. Do not limit yourself to one topic or interest. Be able to walk into a crowded room and be seen. More importantly, be heard.

The Man Commandments

Chapter Four

Wipe your feet at the door

How many times in our lives have we carried the past into our present? How many times have you dragged yesteryear's pain into a new situation and refused to let go of failure, heartache and stay upset from the past? In the moment of grief we refuse to see the light before us. Holding on to discomfort because it reminds us of what we had. Even if it wasn't worth having at all, we refuse to let it go.

In order for men to move on we need definitive answers. We need to know when and where did things go wrong and what part did we play in it all. As men we are taught to mask hardships. We are conditioned to see ourselves as being weak if we are up against an obstacle that we cannot immediately resolve. Why have we adopted this way of thinking as part of our make up? This way of thinking and

The Man Commandments

living is not productive or healthy. It creates an imbalance that affects the way we rationalize all encounters.

When we are at a point in our lives of transitioning from the old to the new we must completely break away from our past. One cannot be productive in their new relationship if they continue to hold onto the difficulties from their prior relationships. You will only frustrate yourself by hindering your ability to appreciate what is new and rewarding. Let the past go. By doing so, you not only open yourself up for emotional growth but also for personal expansion.

This applies to social and personal relationships as well. Past friends and lovers may have temporarily tarnished your concern and affection for them. Whether it is due to a falling out or that the love has simply withered away. Do not allow these emotions to block the way you view future relationships. In many cases, most men may inadvertently

The Man Commandments

wear the burden of their failed relationships. Unfortunately they will carry these bruised emotions into the next one.

Heartache does something to us that in simpler terms is damaging to our self-esteem. We often feel defeated. This in turn creates a sense of self-pity. This state of loathing may carry on unintentionally and you may find yourself coming across to other women or people in general as moody or one with a negative outlook. This is something that is crippling to a man's soul and it is imperative that he shakes this.

At times we may appear strong as steel when it comes to experiencing pain and grief. Little does the woman know that this is a façade. If we focused and came to grips with this pain, we would realize it is the same pain and grief that propels us toward enlightenment and clarity. This gives us the strength to endure whatever is to follow. Looking

The Man Commandments

within myself I realize that I have hid emotions in many cases simply to save myself from being hurt.

The wall that I would put up inadvertently would make me become numb and emotionally cold in many cases. At times I would act distant to some women while being compassionate to others. I considered this behavioral pattern as delegating my emotions in percentages. The women that I truly felt were genuine I gave them all of me. Women that I was unsure of or whom I considered a passerby, I would give less than 50% of my time and energy.

I once before assumed that this mode of operation was best for me. In essence, it was the emotional death of me. For I should never have given my time or energy to one who is not deserving of it. As men we have to think logically and not selfishly. Acting in accordance with self-gratification

The Man Commandments

and wanting to please our eyes and flesh while disregarding and disrespecting our soul is what will jam us up most of the time. It is very easy to waste your time with the wrong person. It's even easier to convince yourself that the wrong person is the right one for you. In the midst of this emotional journey, keep in mind that all responsibility falls upon you. Waiting for a blow out is like being a masochist so do not complain later for what you failed to act on.

Instead of expecting emotional pain and looking forward to dilemmas, you should focus on removing yourself from relationships that bring about such. The longer you stay in a toxic relationship the more resentful you become and the more disappointed you become with yourself for not believing you were deserving of more. This can bring about an emotional shift that in some cases lead to depression. Remaining in this depressed state of being will also bring forth shortness in temper and arguments. This is never

The Man Commandments

good. Beating up on yourself for not reacting to the signs of trouble will have you agitated and rude to your lover/spouse. You will also lash out at one another because you failed to be honest with yourselves from the beginning. Admit to yourself that liking an individual is not the same as loving them and being attracted to a person is not the same as wanting to share in their life.

These are the basic fundamentals of relationship building that many overlook. We take a nice smile over a nice personality. We appreciate a nice ass more than a loving embrace. By the time we are in deep emotionally, we feel jaded and too full of false pride to throw in the towel. So what do we do? We beat each other up emotionally until the other cannot take anymore and bows out gracefully.

Though you may have finally escaped that mistake, inadvertently what you have created within yourself and

The Man Commandments

partner are two dysfunctional people. You have put so much energy into proving how you were wrong for each other that it is hard to imagine how you could be right for anyone else. You carry this baggage of disappointment around with you. Dropping pieces of it off in the laps of each and every person you meet. This is how the cycle of abuse continues.

The only true way of salvaging self is by wiping your feet at the door before entering something new. Be alone. There is nothing wrong with accepting that time is needed to realign yourself. Accept the fact that you may have flaws. Deal with them before making them another person's problem.

Dismissing full account of your pros and cons not only makes you an emotionally irresponsible person, it shows your lack of concern for others. We want to be the best we

The Man Commandments

can be and this should be the energy we give off. We want to lead being genuine and with love. This is what we deserve and in order to be deserving of such we must be willing to give the same. If you operate on this accord better days are ahead of you.

The Man Commandments

FOOD FOR THOUGHT

To ensure a happy and healthy life you must have fun. Incorporate laughter in every day that you rise. There is no joy in socializing if you are going to focus on every little thing that made you mad hours before. Let it go and live in the moment.

The Man Commandments

Chapter Five

NOW!

How grand is it that we can be the recipients of words of enlightenment. As I write these words of life and love, I reflect on the days when I said to myself that my people are missing out on what I have to share. For there was a time when writing my thoughts down were the last thing on my mind. Being busy with projects, out and about throughout the community, and simply being a family man. All of these things that kept me quite occupied. Never the less I've always kept in mind that I must return to self.

"Appreciating and loving this life of mine."

The time is NOW! Right now at this very moment is the greatest moment of our lives. It is at this moment that you have the opportunity to dictate your next move. You have the pleasure of planning your future. Outlining your own

The Man Commandments

path with a blissful imagination. This very moment that you are living in is one of infinite possibilities.

Yesterday's mishaps may have prepared you for today but this day shall bring forth insight that may last you forever. You are a wiser and brighter person for the lessons learned. You are eager and full of vigor. There is nothing that can derail you from the track that you're on. If you choose to quit accept that it is at your own will. Nothing more. Knowing this should propel you even further for it is YOU that are the source of your own drive.

Contemplation. Erase this word and concept from your vocabulary. It is a word of old. We second-guess nothing in the NOW. In the NOW we say YES when we would have said no. We are sure about where we are headed and what we expect out of this life.

The Man Commandments

No longer are we to wonder what the next rising sun will bring. This day we rise with our eyes on the prize with a plan to execute our mission with accuracy and efficiency. Not for one second will we doubt our own strengths. We have tapped into the inner core of our own spiritual being and it has reassured us that all is fine. I repeat all is fine.

In the NOW we smile with a purpose. We have come to embrace the fact that happiness is NOT an option. Happiness is our God given right. It is who we are without external influences. Being happy is not an application that can be turned on and off depending on the circumstances placed upon us.

Being happy is synonymous with being alive. The act of being, feeling, living, laughing, loving, learning and growing is the definition of NOW. This is life in motion, never ending and everlasting.

The Man Commandments

My Brothers, I ask that you take this moment as you read these words and truly embrace your current state of being. Whether you are upset, confused, depressed or stressed. Please keep in mind that you are the force that drives your physical being in the direction that you want to go. You are the beholder of your spirituality and higher power. One must learn to harness this power on a daily basis and not only when times seem dark and gloomy.

Tapping into this higher power on a daily basis shall keep you focused and in tune with what is of true importance, YOU. So to all I say that the time is NOW! It is time for all of us to wipe away the tears of yesterday and take ownership of the bright horizon ahead. We are destined for greatness for it is greatness from which we came.

The Man Commandments

FOOD FOR THOUGHT

Let go of this thing called "ego". It's hard to laugh at other people's jokes when you are caught up into yourself.

The Man Commandments

Chapter Six

Man Vs. Woman

Let's stop playing all the emotional games and put all the chips on the table. Right now it gets real. This is the chapter I shed light on behalf of us men that rarely get it's proper acknowledgement, the true and vulnerable side.

Men, Who are we? Why do we do what we do? Is it because society is set up in our favor or is our ego set up by this society? We are every element that is life itself. We are comprised of the negative images this world puts in front of us and on us. We choose to use our intellect to decipher the good from the bad, the truth from a lie, the real from the fake, and proceed accordingly. We walk upright and bare the burden for negative stereotypes placed upon us. Yet with all of this stated it is our ego that determines whom we shall be for this day. WE, the men that go out of our way to prove ourselves, do this specifically to distinguish

The Man Commandments

ourselves. Men that are content with being slackers and loafers do not care about how others feel about them. Their ego has masked their concern and emotions. Either you understand them or you don't.

In many cases, it is the men that are good to women that receive the third degree. Women will attempt to bombard good men with a million questions to see if he is the real deal. While on the contrary (in one's head) the egotistical and vain man will have a more relaxed encounter with certain women. In today's clouded society an over inflated ego is considered confidence. To some women this means if you're not full of yourself then it must mean that you are not sure of yourself. Though these are extremely two different dynamics, it has created confusion between today's men and women.

The Man Commandments

When we feel that we are financially and mentally superior over that woman, we correspond with her in an infantile manner. We do so as if we're doing her a favor by talking to her. When we meet a woman that is equal to us (financially & mentally), we tend to challenge her intellect and give her the run around. Why do we do this? It is because power respects power.

We are attracted to what we cannot manipulate instantly. The challenge is a turn on because it stimulates our ego and secondly, because we want to maintain our advantage. We want to be desired by that woman, but inadvertently there are times that we turn her off. The ego loses.

A woman without a car may find a man with a car to be an asset. A man with a car may find a woman without a car not as an equal and vice versa. This is an egotistical leverage. By not wanting or needing her assistance, this

The Man Commandments

conditions us to believe a woman without a car becomes a liability. Someone for us to take care of and tend to. In one way or another we know that she is dependent upon us. This is how the weak male mind operates.

Men, you need to know that it is hard being all for self and for her. It is hard for many men to maintain their beliefs and standards when society and some women do not appreciate you. You must understand that the world that we live in is not a fair and just one. For every good step forward we are tested and pushed back two steps. When your focus is to stay away from temptations, society places images that are strategically geared to entice and stimulate the mind to lure you in. Today we call them Instagram models.

The Man Commandments

The mind game #1

Regardless if you honor and cherish the bond you have with your woman, there are women who will test your will and love for your spouse. They will do this not because they are truly into you but because they want to see if they can get into your head, bed, and life. To break a good man is an ultimate high for certain women. All this woman may want to prove is that men are all the same, "DOGS". Little does she know that she is far from being accurate in her assumptions.

Being one with a nature of disrupting the peace in an established relationship is the "DOG" or as most would state, the "BITCH". A woman testing a man's commitment is no better than the man who succumbs to her advances. There is no such thing as proving all men to be dogs when a dog is teaching the lesson.

The Man Commandments

Where does the accountability come in when individuals act with the intent of deception? Is this dismissed in the sake of proving a point while all along disregarding one's own integrity?

The mind game #2

There are women that accuse men who choose not to stray from their woman to be less than masculine or real. There use to be a saying women would utter when their advances were turned down. They would say, "Oh, he's scared of this pussy". I know some are laughing at that line because you know I'm telling the truth. When we as men have this as an obstacle in front of us, how can you question a man's stance? Women, it is your own sisters that are bringing you down with their disregard for commitment.

Men that have decided to take care of their family and whether the storm, I commend you. I consider myself a

The Man Commandments

good man. In reality, it is not even my place me to label myself as such in a relationship. That is for the woman in my life to do. Being a good man means that I am accountable, loving, attentive and I take responsibility for my actions and the energy that I share with her.

Not for one minute will I say or portray to be a perfect man. At times I get on women's nerves. There are times we as men may get to the point where we question where do we go from here. This is in part due to individuals searching for oneness amongst each other. Does this NOT make you a good man? No, it makes you human.

One is capable of being right, wrong, good, bad and indifferent. It is a conscious decision that men make to live right and just for the woman in their life. This is what separates boys from the men. It is the reasoning that we use which allows us to think as a man or a child. It is the

The Man Commandments

teachings of wise and knowledgeable elders that were laid out before us to build us up. These teachings are to positively shape our minds and guide us toward nobility and truth.

I have two children; a son and a daughter. I want them to know the difference between the truth in life and the lies that live within and around us. Having a clear outlook on life is what makes me an observant man. I want what is understood to be the truth, not just for me but also for others. I am who I am. A man by all means.

To all true and dedicated men, stay focused and on point. We are faced against many evils on this earth. Succumbing to anything beneath greatness is not in our blood. Following the masses, being reckless, deceitful, and disrespectful is common practice for most. This behavior will never be mistaken for the true nature and purpose of

The Man Commandments

man. We are, and should continue, to strive to be the definition of what men are which are reflections of The Most High.

The Man Commandments

FOOD FOR THOUGHT

Being a man and convincing someone of your manhood are two different things. Never feel the need to prove who you are. Simply be the best man that you can.

The Man Commandments

Chapter Seven

Chivalry isn't dead; it took a back seat to false independence.

Men of today have such a complicated life when it pertains to dealing with our counterparts, women. When I state that it's complicated, I do not mean this in a negative way. I simply mean that being a man's man in today's climate of the "INDEPENDENT WOMAN", we as men find ourselves in unnecessary power struggles. We have transitioned from the era of men generally being the leader to women marching to the drum of their own beat. Though nothing is wrong with the independent woman, the egos of both man and woman have clashed today more than ever.

The curbside affect

The suggestion of women not walking near the curb is an old fashioned custom. Today, in a time when some women will tell you that they will walk wherever they choose may confuse some of the men whom embrace this custom. She

The Man Commandments

has not taken into regards that this precaution is done for their own safety and honor. As my elders explained it to me, allowing a woman to walk near the curb meant one or two things. For one, it meant that you were exploiting her or advertising her to those in cars passing. The same way a Pimp would do to his Prostitutes. Secondly, it meant that you were subjecting that woman to possible danger. In the event that a car would jump the curb, it would be her that is hit first for she's the closest to the curb. Men should walk on the outer side to be a barrier for their woman's protection.

In no shape or form should this precaution to be taken as a controlling measure. Most men are groomed to protect. Men who act accordingly should not be mistaken as those who seek to dictate or control. This is one of the many grey areas that exist today between women and men. Protection should not be interpreted as aid to defenseless woman.

The Man Commandments

Moving forward

Women have evolved in our society at a rewarding and outstanding rate. Women lead in receiving college degrees and in most Black households are typically the highest earning breadwinner. This being a factor and part of the modern woman's independence plays a large part in how we associate. One may believe that the slightest suggestion from a man may be perceived as a power struggle. One of those common ideas is to have the woman to submit which is a false assumption indeed.

Although being caring and protective is not the same as controlling, anything that may come across as indicating what may be best for that woman may conflict with her sense of independence. It all depends on how you approach the situation. Never take the stance as being the sole bearer of logic. This is where clarity must come into play.

The Man Commandments

Let's recap

Men; we are to take responsibility for the well being of our women. Allowing them to walk near the curb is a no go. It is never about being in control or dictating where a woman can or cannot walk. It is done to protect her physically as well as her honor. A logical woman understands this. Regardless of her being independent and capable of caring for herself all women want to feel protected.

Women respect men who cherish and honor them. They will appreciate any and all gestures made in attempt to hold them in high regard. As independent and confident as a woman may be, a strong man is whom they desire. They desire a man that compliments their accolades, not one who is overshadowed by them. When a woman feels that she is the head of the two this is when your attempts of chivalry will not matter to her.

The Man Commandments

Men love being the "MAN" but if he is incapable of making that woman feel like "The" woman then all efforts have failed. Open that door for her; pull out that chair for her as she is seated. Carry the grocery bags inside and never allow her to bare the burden when in your company. There are women today that may come across as unimpressed by your gestures of chivalry, so what. Continue to be the man that you are. That very woman will know the difference between you and a man who does not hold her in the same regards.

The breakdown

A man viewed as insufficient cannot demonstrate acts of chivalry for certain women and be appreciated for such act. Some women who are in a better financial situation may think it's your "JOB" to open doors for her and to cater to her. They may not equate your acts as chivalry.

The Man Commandments

An insufficient man in her eyes may only be doing what she thinks he should. By doing such, she may think this is to compensate for his shortcomings.

This in itself is part of the great power struggle that men and women of today go through. Respect and love are provisional, solely based on and rationed according to what the man brings to the table. If you're incapable of paying for dinner then it's highly improbable that you'll get to lay with her. This may not be the case for all women today but for women of substance, more than likely. This may be one of the few times chivalry may matter.

The Man Commandments

FOOD FOR THOUGHT

Never let it be said that love is a sin because LOVE is the main component of inner soul mastery. When true lovers master it, destinies are searched for and discovered.

The Man Commandments

Chapter Eight.

BLACK LOVE

If I may, allow me to state this loud & clear- **BLACK LOVE IS NOT EXTINCT**. The proper definition is not defined by words of a song but of actions by the individual. Extinct as many may believe is an incorrect assumption. Those of us that may be in love tend to adapt to the emotional state we're placed in. This is in accordance to our social relevance or relationship status. If we feel happy in our personal lives we will transfer that energy over into our relationships. If we are feeling ourselves due to attention given by multiple people, then our arrogance will tend to dictate when and how deep we become committed.

When we are not happy with ourselves we carry that energy into our encounters with others. We become clouded in our judgment and entertain the first person that makes us smile. Unfortunately, those who are not in tune with self will

The Man Commandments

allow everything outside of self, their nature, and their spouse to define what love is. Allowing others to define what are the key components to a successful marriage may not be beneficial in many cases. What works for some may not work for all.

This goes without saying that everyone's intentions are not the same. Today some marry simply to say that they are married. Many do it to give off the illusion as being wanted. They want others to see them as one that is capable of being married, desired. They want to be viewed as someone another has come to terms with and are deeply in love with.

Although I rarely hear of true love being expressed publicly in today's society, it actually exists. Many may feel jaded from failed relationships hindering themselves from gravitating to a possibly new and true love. Today's young

The Man Commandments

men and women's definition of love comes with contingencies. This is why the state of BLACK LOVE & MARRIAGE may appear synthetic to most. There are men that opt to not marry if the woman already has a child or children. There are women that opt to not marry if the man's credit score is below 700. The fundamentals of love, Black LOVE, have taken a backseat to a distorted social criteria, paperwork, and contractual formalities.

This way of living is leaving Black enthusiasts asking where's the love at? Black love is a beautiful concept. It can only be embraced as such when we receive our counterparts as beautiful and a necessity to our existence. I'm not referring to the world's standards. I am referring to that deep, spiritual, and inner feeling. That reassuring feeling within that warms your essence when in the presence of each other. The love and compassion that is born from a state of harmony. A feeling that only you can

The Man Commandments

share with your spouse. Never looking to judge or rationalize your level of love through the eyes of your friends or family. All that matter is the imagery of love as seen through your eyes only. The soul stirring moment when you realize that you would share your last grain of salt and up to every dollar you have with this person. There is an infinite amount of possibility when it comes to emotional growth without fear of ridicule.

When you have these ingredients that I've mentioned as the foundation, BLACK LOVE and Black Marriage is synonymous. Take away the frivolous concerns of he or she being cute in the eyes of your friends. Stop being overly concerned about what is the make of their car and what is their BMI. All of that is synthetic, trivial bullshit that has nothing to do with love or compatibility. Master self and you two will become masters as ONE.

The Man Commandments

BLACK LOVE in its purest form is the greatest feeling ever. Essential as the sun is to every life form in existence. Our cohesiveness is what continues us going. For if we begin to give up on BLACK LOVE, then we have given up on humanity itself. Think about that.

BLACK LOVE IS NOT

Black love is NOT the psychological abuse placed upon your spouse because you believe they are to bare the burden of your mistakes. Black love is NOT crushing the dreams and stepping on the ideas of a loved one. Black love is not fear of supporting them because the possibility of their success threatens you. This is not love, it is envy. Where there is envy hate will eventually manifest.

This hate is the fuel for verbal and physical abuse that runs rampant in many of our homes. A hate and disorder that must be addressed and gotten rid of. Black love is unique,

The Man Commandments

unlike anything else in the world. When this is compromised and ripped away piece by piece the same effect is taking place on our lives. When you speak down to your spouse what happens is you negate their existence.

If the person they seek refuge in now becomes the one they fear then their world becomes upside down. They are forced to fight the world on two fronts just to stay alive which is the world outside of their home and the chaos within. This is not the embodiment of love, yet alone, BLACK LOVE. This is a sure disaster, one that many face and deal with on a daily basis.

Black love should not be a label for neglect and pain in which one lives through simply because of our commonality. There is no peace in chanting BLACK LOVE and KEEP THE BLACK FAMILY TOGETHER if either party is emotionally destroying the other. Black love

The Man Commandments

is deeper than looking inseparable in pictures. Black love is an unspoken bond, level of respect, commitment, solidarity, and trust that not even your best Mahogany card could capture in words. Black love is what kept our many nations together.

Black love is EVERYTHING and don't you ever forget it.

The Man Commandments

CONCLUSION

As I depart I conclude with a definite feeling of assurance. I am also confident that these pages have guided you all, man and woman alike. Regardless of your stance, agree or disagree. Allow this book to be the reason for an open discussion on the chapters and various topics. Be willing to communicate, receive advice, and criticism without taking offense. Life is for the living and in this life we are learning on a continuous basis. Each moment is a learning experience, a lesson. These lessons shall either shape us for the better or expose a side of us that may need fine-tuning.

The Man Commandments

DEDICATION

To my mother; Barbara Jean-Russell McKinney. May you rest in everlasting peace. You instilled extraordinary qualities in me. It is because of you that I am who I am.

To my father; Michael A.H. McKinney. Thank you for being an example of what a man should aspire to become. You taught me how to carry myself with dignity. This is something I shall never waver from.

To my sister & brother-in-law; Stephanie and Kenny Turner. Thank you both for your continuous support. I know I am in your prayers daily and this is what keeps me going. Thank you for always being in my corner.

To my sister; Daphanie Ann. May you rest in everlasting peace. I know you're proud of me. I am pleased with

The Man Commandments

knowing this. Trust and believe your name will live forever through me.

To my nieces and nephews; Tyrone (Ty-Ty), Dominique, Dontè, Te'ana and Joel. I love you all more than you'll ever know. Regardless the distance in miles between us I'll always be right there for you.

To my brothers; Charlton & Kyle McKinney. You two are the best brothers a man could have. You're always there when I need you. It's an honor to be your big brother. I am extremely proud of you both.

To my beloved children; Ieszan Siekiem-Kontom McKinney and Isis Syleen-Kontom McKinney. You two are the main reason that I do everything in my power to be the best human being. All that matters in my world is setting great examples for you both to follow. Daddy loves

The Man Commandments

you. To the McKinney & Russell family, I love you all. Thank you for your love and support.

The Man Commandments

ACKNOWLEDGEMENTS

Much love and respect to the following: Tashana Jackson and her son Shakir, The Miller Family, The Grant Family, Charleston S.C., Memphis TN, N.A. Rock, Bed-Stuy, Greene Avenue, Lexington Avenue, Brooklyn NY, Richmond VA, D.C., Maryland, Irvington, NJ, and Pittsburgh, PA.

My inner circle: Rasheen, Frederick, Keith, Carlos, Michelle, Joseph, Marlon, Wise, Anthony, Lee, Infinite, Shawn (Black), Derrick, Darius, Lael Rogers, Kendu Rogers, Gary Rogers (RIP), Gerald Rogers, Johnny & Karen Henderson, Blackjack, D'andria, Tahitia, Chanel, Lewis, Vincent, Lil Shawn, Stack, Iron, Forever, Jermaine, Deucy, Miz, Murdock (RIP), Saladin Shabazz, Born, Ty-Quan, Lywan, Cire, L.C., Jamar, Ms. Small, J. Spears,

The Man Commandments

Sh. Johnson, J. Buchanan, R. Bush, D. Carter, T. Crawford, Dr. Channing Porter Moreland, Bernadine Johnson, Cassandra Stephens, O. Ford, A. Meyers, P. Moore,

Austin Vanbrackle, NYDOC, TABLEOFKINGZ, Jibriel Muhammad, Niya Muhammad, Shahidah Rasheed, Rose Muhammad, Gary "Master G" Clark, Gary Thomas, GT Brand, Inshallah Clothing, C. Grooms, TEN G PUBLISHING, Sir Ibu, Anthony Robinson (T. Starks), NOI, 5% Nation of Gods & Earths and most importantly YOU.

www.ingramcontent.com/pod-product-compliance
Lightning Source LLC
Chambersburg PA
CBHW032210040426
42449CB00005B/529